ARTS and CRAFTS

PHOTOGRAPHS BY PETER MAGUBANE

TEXT BY SANDRA KLOPPER

Published by Struik Publishers
(a division of New Holland Publishing (South Africa) (Pty) Ltd)

London • Cape Town • Sydney • Auckland

Garfield House
86 Edgware Road
W2 2EA London
United Kingdom

14 Aquatic Drive
Frenchs Forest
NSW 2086
Australia

80 McKenzie Street
Cape Town 8001
South Africa

218 Lake Road
Northcote, Auckland
New Zealand

Website: www.struik.co.za

ISBN 1 86872 516 2

Design director   Janice Evans
Publishing manager   Annlerie van Rooyen
Design   Illana Fridkin
Managing editor   Lesley Hay-Whitton
Proofreader   Glynne Newlands
French translator   Jean-Paul Houssière
German translator   Friedel Herrmann

Reproduction by Hirt & Carter (Cape) Pty Ltd
Printed and bound by APP Printers, Singapore

Copyright © in published edition Struik Publishers 2001
Copyright © in photographs Peter Magubane 2001
Copyright © in text Sandra Klopper 2001

10 9 8 7 6 5 4 3 2 1

All rights reserved. No part of this publication may be reproduced, stored in a retrieval system or transmitted, in any form or by any means, electronic, mechanical, photocopying, recording or otherwise, without the prior written permission of the copyright owners.

Front cover: Ndebele muralist Francina Ndimande at her homestead.
Back cover: A clay sculpture by Venda artist Noria Mabasa.
Page 1: Baskets produced in the Hlabisa district of KwaZulu-Natal.
Page 2 (left): Ndebele muralist Esther Mahlangu.
Page 2 (right): A Venda drum used in female initiation ceremonies.
Page 3 (left): Bantwane dolls.
Page 3 (right): Ndebele woman preparing a gourd for use as a vessel.
Opposite: Men at the Sotho cultural village near Golden Gate in the Free State.
Page 6: Ndebele artist displaying a craft piece made for the tourist market.

INTRODUCTION

Rural South African communities still produce vibrant art forms similar to those practised in pre-colonial times. Using indigenous materials such as clay, wood and grass, they make beautiful, often richly decorated artefacts for ritual and household purposes. In keeping with traditions established by earlier communities who acquired imported glass beads in exchange for cattle and ivory, many craft specialists still buy beads to produce various forms of dress and adornment for festive occasions like weddings and coming-out ceremonies of young male and female initiates.

In addition to these older art forms, locally made plastic beads and recycled objects like the tops of Coca Cola bottles are commonly used to make garments and artefacts associated with events that mark important moments in the lives of rural traditionalists. The remarkable creativity of these traditionalists is also seen in the production of murals on homestead walls, and in ephemeral art forms like the body painting practices employed in certain initiation contexts.

Today, as in the past, men work as carvers, while women make beadwork and clay pots. Historically entrenched divisions of labour are, however, often no longer observed. This is especially evident in the fact that today very few men still weave baskets. The increasingly dominant role women play in the production of this and other art forms can be ascribed to the need to generate income in outlying rural areas where many of these women continue to live, raising children and engaging in subsistence farming while their husbands work in large urban centres.

Although women still make clay pots and clothing and adornment for local use, development agencies have become actively involved in encouraging them to produce work for outside markets. Because of these attempts to help women achieve greater financial independence, the artistic traditions of rural craft specialists have repeatedly been revitalized through the impact on producers of different consumer groups with sometimes vastly incompatible needs. The need for economic independence has also led increasing numbers of women to learn skills that in some cases were associated with particular families. The reason for this is that both male and female craft specialists commonly tend to pass their artistic knowledge on to their sons and daughters.

INTRODUCTION

Les communautés rurales produisent les mêmes formes d'art éclatant que celles remontant à l'époque pré-coloniale. Utilisant des matériaux ordinaires, comme la terre glaise, du bois et des herbes sèches, on continue à créer des objets bien souvent richement ornés, qui sont utilisés dans les cérémonies rituelles ou pour les tâches ménagères. Suivant les traditions remontant à l'époque quand les communautés troquaient leur bétail et de l'ivoire contre des perles de verres apportées par les pionniers, de nombreux artistes continuent d'utiliser des perles pour créer des parures et des costumes qui seront portés lors de célébrations comme les mariages ou les festivités se rattachant à l'initiation des jeunes.

Des formes d'art traditionnelles, les objets et costumes sont souvent ornés avec des perles de plastique et des matériaux de recyclage comme des capsules de bouteilles de Coca-Cola, des épingles à cheveux et des accessoires automobiles. L'imagination de ces traditionalistes est mise en évidence dans les peintures recouvrant leurs murs, et dans les motifs peints avec de l'argile à même la peau de ceux qui participent aux cérémonies d'initiation.

Comme dans le passé, la sculpture est faite par les hommes et ce sont les femmes qui travaillent avec les perles et qui modèlent la glaise. Ce traditionnel partage des tâches n'est plus tellement respecté: très peu d'hommes tressent encore des paniers en herbes sèches, cette activité étant maintenant l'apanage des femmes qui sont de plus en plus amenées à la production d'objets d'artisanat. En effet, alors que les hommes travaillent à la ville, la responsabilité des femmes de la campagne, outre d'élever les enfants et cultiver la terre, est de produire un revenu pour subvenir aux besoins familiaux.

Alors que les femmes produisent des pots de terre cuite, des costumes et des parures pour leur propre usage, des agences de développement commencent à les encourager dans la production commerciale. Dans ces tentatives d'aider les femmes à atteindre une plus grande autonomie financière, les traditions des artisans sont continuellement revitalisées par les demandes d'un marché qui ne sont pas toujours compatibles. Le besoin de devenir financièrement indépendantes a poussé de plus en plus de femmes à adopter des techniques venant d'autres communautés, techniques qui, étant passées d'une génération à l'autre, ont tendance à rester l'exclusivité de cette communauté en particulier.

EINFÜHRUNG

Bei der Landbevölkerung in Südafrika floriert noch immer lebendiges Kunsthandwerk, wie es schon vor der Kolonialzeit ausgeübt wurde. Unter Verwendung einheimischer Materialien wie Ton, Holz und Stroh werden weiterhin schön abgearbeitete und oftmals reich verzierte Artikel für rituelles Brauchtum und als Hausrat angefertigt. Früher wurden importierte Glasperlen im Tauschhandel für Rinder und Elfenbein erstanden, und auch heutzutage werden Perlen in Kleidung und Schmuck verarbeitet für festliche Anlässe wie Hochzeiten und die Einführung männlicher und weiblicher Initianden in die Gesellschaft.

Abgesehen von diesen überlieferten Handarbeiten benutzt man heute auch Plastikperlen und Objekte wie Coladeckel, um Kleidungsstücke und sinnbildliche Artikel für besondere Anlässe im Leben der traditionsverbundenen Landbevölkerung herzustellen. Die beeindruckende Kreativität dieser Traditionalisten zeigt sich auch in Wandmalereien an Heimstätten, sowie in der zwar kurzlebigen, aber künstlerischen Körperverzierung mancher Initianden.

Auch heute noch fertigen Männer die Schnitzereien an, während Frauen Perlenarbeiten und Tongefäße herstellen, aber oftmals wird diese historisch gewachsene Arbeitsteilung nicht mehr beachtet. Männer fertigen kaum noch Korbarbeiten an; diese werden nahezu ausschließlich von Frauen gearbeitet. Die führende Rolle, die Frauen heute in der Herstellung von kunstgewerblichen Handarbeiten einnehmen, läßt sich darauf zurückführen, daß sich Frauen, die weiterhin auf dem Lande leben und dort ihre Kinder aufziehen und Subsistenzwirtschaft betreiben, eigenes Einkommen verschaffen müssen, da die Männer zur Arbeit in die Großstädte abwandern.

Obwohl die Frauen noch immer Tongefäße, Bekleidung und Schmuck für den Lokalbedarf anfertigen, sind Entwicklungsgesellschaften aktiv, um sie für die Produktion von Handarbeiten für andere Absatzmärkte zu interessieren. Diese Ansätze zielen darauf ab, Frauen größere finanzielle Unabhängigkeit zu ermöglichen und haben eine Wiederbelebung ländlicher Talente hervorgerufen. Der Drang nach wirtschaftlicher Unabhängigkeit hat Frauen auch dazu gebracht, sich Fertigkeiten anzunehmen, für die ihre Familien bekannt sind, da männliche wie weibliche Künstler ihr Können gern an die eigenen Kinder weitergeben.

The practice of carving artefacts associated with rituals is common throughout Africa. Although the drums and other musical instruments used on these occasions are invariably made by men, in female initiation ceremonies they are always played by women.

L'usage de sculpter des objets liés aux rituels est répandu dans toute l'Afrique. Bien que les tambours et autres instruments utilisés lors des cérémonies soient fabriqués par les hommes, ce sont les femmes qui les jouent pour l'initiation des jeunes filles.

In ganz Afrika schnitzt man künstlerische Artikel von ritueller Bedeutung. Zwar werden Trommeln und andere Musikinstrumente für diese Anlässe ausnahmslos von den Männern gemacht, aber bei weiblichen Initiationszeremonien werden sie nur von Frauen gespielt.

The carved drums played at events like weddings and the coming-out ceremonies of diviners vary considerably in size and shape. But the cured skin membranes stretched across their tops are always secured with the aid of large wooden pegs.

Les tambours sculptés que l'on voit aux mariages et autres cérémonies varient considérablement en forme et en volume. La peau d'animal tendue sur l'extrémité est toujours attachée avec de grosses chevilles de bois.

Die geschnitzten Trommeln, die anläßlich von Hochzeiten und Einführungszeremonien geschlagen werden, unterscheiden sich in Form und Größe. Aber die gegerbten Tierfelle, mit denen sie bespannt sind, werden immer mit großen hölzernen Klammern befestigt.

Traditionalists today commonly make musical instruments from recycled materials like can and bottle tops (*right*) to create various kinds of percussive sounds. Similarly, large paint tins are sometimes turned into drums (*opposite*), but these tins are also used to carry water from distant rivers, and to store staple dry foods like sugar and maize meal, especially where people do not have access to the clay containers produced by rural potters.

Les traditionalistes contemporains fabriquent couramment des instruments à percussion avec des matériaux de recyclage, comme des boîtes de fer-blanc et des capsules de bouteilles (*à droite*). De même, on verra des bidons de peinture tenant lieu de tambours (*ci-contre*); ces mêmes bidons servent à transporter l'eau et à entreposer des aliments secs comme le maïs et le sucre, par ceux qui ne possèdent pas de pots de terre cuite.

Heute verwenden die Traditionalisten durch Abfallnutzung häufig Artikel wie Flaschenverschlüsse und Büchsen zur Herstellung von Musikinstrumenten (*rechts*), denen unterschiedliche Schlagzeugtöne entlockt werden. Desgleichen werden große Farbkübel zu Trommeln umfunktioniert (*gegenüber*). Aber diese Behälter werden auch zum Wassertragen oder zur Aufbewahrung von Lebensmitteln wie Zucker und Maismehl benutzt, besonders dort, wo Tongefäße von ländlichen Töpfern nicht erhältlich sind.

The use of locally manufactured musical instruments (*opposite*) and commercially produced brass horns and trumpets (*right*) is so widespread that outsiders sometimes form the impression that rural communities no longer treasure long-established traditions, including the production of indigenous art forms. Although it is true that many of these practices have been eroded, for example through the impact of migrant labour, traditionalists still value the skills of local craftsmen and -women.

Le mariage entre les instruments de musique indigènes (*ci-contre*) avec ceux d'origine occidentale comme les cornets et trompettes (*à droite*), est tellement répandu que les étrangers pourraient penser que les communautés rurales ne respectent plus les anciennes traditions, y compris les autres formes d'art. Il est vrai que bien de ces anciennes pratiques se sont érodées, par exemple, dû au travail saisonnier, mais les traditionalistes chérissent toujours le talent des artisans locaux.

Einheimische Musikinstrumente (*gegenüber*) und die im Handel erhältlichen Trompeten und Hörner aus Messing treten so oft gleichzeitig in Erscheinung, daß Außenstehende mitunter den Eindruck gewinnen, die Landbevölkerung schenkt mittlerweile ihren althergebrachten Traditionen, wie den einheimischen Kunstarten, wenig Bedeutung. Zugegebenerweise sind viele Bräuche im Zerfall begriffen, etwa durch die Auswirkung der Wanderarbeit, aber Traditionalisten schätzen durchaus noch das Können der einheimischen Künstler und Künstlerinnen.

Among the Tswana, and elsewhere in South Africa, male initiates receive one or more carved sticks in recognition of their transition to manhood. To this day, these sticks are sometimes surmounted by figurative details but, because they are often used in stick fighting competitions, most end in variously sized knobs. While many of these knobs are beautifully decorated, as in the past others are fashioned from the gnarled roots of trees.

Chez les Tswanas, comme partout en Afrique du Sud, les garçons reçoivent un ou plusieurs bâtons sculptés lors de leur initiation. Souvent, l'extrémité comporte une figurine, qui à la longue s'abîme et se déforme en pommeau, les bâtons étant souvent utilisés dans des concours de combat. Alors que de nombreux pommeaux sont joliment ornés, d'autres, comme dans le passé, sont faits de racines d'arbres noueuses.

Bei den Tswana, wie auch anderswo in Südafrika, erhalten männliche Initianden in Anerkennung ihres Übergangs zum Mannestum einen oder mehrere geschnitzte Stöcke. Bis zum heutigen Tag sind manche mit kunstvollen Schnitzereien versehen, da die Stöcke aber häufig für Stockkämpfe benutzt werden, enden die meisten in Knäufen unterschiedlicher Größe. Manche dieser Knäufe sind schön verziert, während andere wie ehedem aus knubbeligen Baumwurzeln angefertigt werden.

Although locally carved sticks are still used in some areas, contemporary initiates sometimes carry cheaper commercially manufactured examples. At one Bakôpa wedding (*above*), the presents given to the bridegroom's family included an unusual walking stick topped by the handle of a saw.

Au lieu de bâtons sculptés localement, les initiés d'aujourd'hui se procurent parfois des modèles moins chers, produits industriellement. A un mariage bakôpa, parmi les cadeaux offerts à la famille du marié, se trouvait un bâton peu ordinaire dont l'extrémité était surmontée par une poignée de scie.

In manchen Gegenden werden noch örtlich geschnitzte Stöcke benutzt, aber heutige Initianden tragen auch billigere, fabrikmäßig erzeugte. Anläßlich einer Hochzeit bei den Bakôpa enthielten die Geschenke für die Familie des Bräutigams einen ungewöhnlichen Spazierstock mit dem Griff einer Säge.

Venda artist Noria Mabasa makes clay figurines for sale to art collectors. She is also famous for carving images in wood, a medium traditionally reserved for male artists. Many of these comparatively large carvings are fashioned from driftwood.

L'artiste venda Noria Mabasa façonne des figurines de terre cuite pour la revente aux collectionneurs. Elle est aussi renommée pour ses figurines en bois sculpté, un art traditionnellement réservé aux hommes. Ces sculptures sont faites utilisant du bois ramassé le long des rivières.

Noria Mabasa ist eine Venda-Künstlerin, die Tonskulpturen für den Verkauf an Kunstliebhaber anfertigt. Sie ist ebenfalls berühmt für ihre Holzschnitzereien, eine Kunstform die traditionsgemäß männlichen Künstlern vorbehalten war. Viele dieser verhältnismäßig großen Schnitzfiguren sind aus Treibholz angefertigt.

Historically, clay figurines were produced for use in initiation contexts and as fertility dolls, but today many are inspired by Western traditions of portraiture and other non-indigenous sources. Some Ndebele artists also produce caricatures of white politicians raised on makeshift plinths.

Historiquement, les figurines de terre cuite étaient fabriquées pour être utilisées lors des occasions rituelles. De nos jours, elles sont souvent inspirées par l'art du portrait occidental et d'autres sources étrangères. Certains artistes ndebeles façonnent des caricatures de politiciens blancs.

Tonfiguren wurden ursprünglich im Zusammenhang mit der Initiation und als Fruchtbarkeitspuppen hergestellt, aber heutzutage sind die meisten durch westliche Traditionen als Portraits und andere nicht-einheimische Anregungen inspiriert. Einige Ndebele-Künstler fertigen auch Karikaturen weißer Politiker auf Sockeln an.

A long-standing tradition prevails among South African communities of making dolls from beads and other locally available materials, for instance woven grass. Although some of these are used as toys, by far the majority are associated with fertility rites.

La fabrication de poupées utilisant des perles et autres matériaux indigènes comme les herbes tressées et la glaise, est une ancienne tradition parmi les communautés rurales d'Afrique du Sud. Bien que certaines servent de jouets, nombreuses sont celles qui sont liées avec les rites de fertilité.

Der Brauch, Puppen aus Perlen und anderen verfügbaren Stoffen, wie geflochtenem Stroh, anzufertigen, hat bei den Völkern Südafrikas eine lange Tradition. Obwohl einige davon als Spielzeug dienen, wird die überwiegende Mehrheit mit Fruchtbarkeitsriten in Verbindung gebracht.

Fertility dolls, like those made by Bantwane women, are used at wedding ceremonies to divine the bride's chances of having children. In most rural communities, husbands still ascribe enormous value to wives who bear a large number of offspring.

Ces jolies poupées bantwanes sont des symboles de fertilité qui sont utilisés aux cérémonies de mariage pour prédire les chances de la mariée d'avoir des enfants. Dans la plupart des communautés rurales, les maris attribuent une énorme valeur aux femmes qui ont beaucoup d'enfants.

Fruchtbarkeitspuppen, wie diese der Bantwane, geben bei der Hochzeitsfeier Anlaß zu Weissagungen über die potentielle Fruchtbarkeit der Braut. In den meisten ländlichen Gemeinschaften messen Ehemänner noch immer solchen Frauen den höchsten Wert zu, die eine große Anzahl Kinder gebären.

Although some dolls continue to be used in ritual contexts, many are now made for sale to outside buyers. Especially among the Zulu, women commonly produce beaded dolls and figurative groups depicting scenes from the life experiences of the urban white market for which these sculptural tableaux are made.

Bien que certaines poupées soient normalement utilisées pour des occasions rituelles, par exemple lors des mariages, on les fabrique aussi en grand nombre pour la revente. Principalement chez les Zoulous, les femmes font des poupées de perles et créent des groupes figuratifs représentant des scènes de la vie quotidienne des blancs dans un contexte urbain.

Obwohl die meisten Puppen immer noch im Zusammenhang mit Riten eine Rolle spielen, werden viele jetzt zum Verkauf an auswärtige Käufer angefertigt. Besonders bei den Zulu produzieren die Frauen häufig Perlenpuppen und Figurengruppen, die das städtische Leben der Weißen widerspiegeln, denn für diesen Markt werden sie hergestellt.

Because most fertility dolls are covered in beads, the core remains invisible. This core may consist of a variety of materials, such as maize cobs, clay or even, in recent years, jam containers and other recycled objects. The use of some of these materials is informed by symbolic considerations, notably the need to underline associations with nature and therefore fertility.

Etant recouvert de perles, le centre même de la plupart des poupées est invisible. Ce centre pourra être un épi de maïs, de la terre cuite ou même un pot de confiture ou autre objet recyclé. Le choix de certains de ces matériaux est symbolique, résultant notamment de la nécessité de souligner les associations avec la nature, et en conséquence, la fertilité.

Weil die Mehrzahl der Fruchtbarkeitspuppen mit Perlen bedeckt ist, bleibt das Innere unsichtbar. Dieses besteht aus unterschiedlichem Material, wie Maiskolben, Ton, oder neuerdings sogar aus Marmeladenbüchsen und anderen aufgewerteten Abfallprodukten. Manchmal liegen symbolische Überlegungen zugrunde, insbesondere das Bedürfnis, die Beziehung zur Natur und daher zur Fruchtbarkeit zu betonen.

The skirts in which Tsonga dolls are dressed are similar to the layered cloth skirts that are worn by married Tsonga women. They are decorated further with beadwork panels identical to those worn by Tsonga women on special occasions. However, they differ from most other local examples in that their facial features are indicated very simply through the addition of three buttons.

Les poupées tsongas sont habillées de plusieurs couches de jupons, comme les costumes des femmes mariées. Elles sont aussi couvertes d'ornements perlés comme ceux portés par les femmes lors d'occasions spéciales. Contrairement aux autres modèles locaux, les traits du visage sont représentés rudimentairement par trois boutons.

Die Puppen der Tsonga tragen Röcke, die den übereinander getragenen Röcken der verheirateten Frauen nachgeahmt sind. Auch der Perlenschmuck, mit dem sie verziert sind, widerspiegelt den Schmuck, den Frauen zu besonderen Anlässen tragen. Sie unterscheiden sich von anderen Puppen, indem die Gesichter nur durch drei Knöpfe angedeutet werden.

Among the Ndebele, women make dolls carrying firewood on their heads for external buyers. These dolls are decorated with beaded panels and blankets similar to those worn on ritual occasions, but rural women never actually collect wood for domestic use dressed in clothing of this kind. These dolls differ significantly from the more abstract examples traditionally used in ritual contexts (*below*).

Chez les Ndebeles, les femmes fabriquent pour la vente des poupées portant du bois à brûler sur la tête. Elles sont revêtues de couvertures et d'ornements comme ceux portés lors des cérémonies rituelles, bien que les femmes de la campagne ne s'habillent pas de la sorte pour ramasser le bois. Ces poupées sont très différentes des exemplaires traditionnels plus abstraits utilisés pour les rituels (*ci-dessous*).

Für Käufer von auswärts fertigen die Frauen der Ndebele auch Puppen an, die Feuerholz auf dem Kopf tragen. Diese Puppen sind mit Perlenstreifen und Decken bekleidet, wie sie zu rituellen Anlässen getragen werden. Aber Landfrauen würden nie in solch einem Aufzug Holz sammeln für den Hausgebrauch. Diese Puppen unterscheiden sich deutlich von den mehr abstrakt gehaltenen, die in rituellen Zusammenhängen verwendet werden (*unten*).

Regardless of whether they are now made for indigenous use or for outside buyers, dolls often represent married women wearing traditional forms of dress. This is because most dolls of this kind served originally to secure the fertility of these women.

Qu'elles soient fabriquées pour usage local ou pour la revente, les poupées représentent souvent des femmes mariées en costume traditionnel. A l'origine, ces poupées étaient normalement utilisées dans les rituels associés à la fécondité.

Gleichgültig, ob sie nun für einheimischen Gebrauch oder für auswärtige Käufer angefertigt wurden, repräsentieren die Puppen oft verheiratete Frauen in traditioneller Tracht. Ursprünglich sollten nämlich Puppen dieser Art für Fruchtbarkeit bei den Frauen sorgen.

Many indigenous artistic traditions have been adapted to serve the needs of new markets. For example, in the past beads were used to make items of personal adornment. As such, they played a crucial role in underlining social status, notably the age and gender of the wearer. Today, many beadworkers make or cover functional and decorative items for sale to local and foreign tourists.

Nombreuses sont les traditions artisanales qui ont été adaptées pour satisfaire les exigences du marché. Par exemple, dans le passé les ornements perlés étaient créés pour usage personnel. Tels que, ils étaient essentiels pour indiquer la classe sociale du porteur, comme son âge et son sexe. De nos jours, les artisans recouvrent de perles des objets ordinaires pour la revente aux touristes.

Viele einheimische Kunstarten sind den neuen Märkten angepaßt worden. Früher wurden beispielsweise Perlen für persönliche Schmuckartikel verwendet. Als solche spielten sie eine wichtige Rolle, um den gesellschaftlichen Stand – besonders Alter und Geschlecht – der Trägerin oder des Trägers zu unterstreichen. Heutzutage werden auch Gebrauchsgegenstände und Zierat mit Perlen verkleidet und Touristen aus dem In- und Ausland zum Kauf angeboten.

Working with brass and copper wire, men historically wove decorative patterns on sticks and staffs. In the mid-20th century these techniques were adapted by migrant labourers who began using plastic covered telephone wire to make items for sale to outsiders.

Historiquement, les hommes ornaient leurs bâtons avec des tresses en fils de cuivre et de laiton. Vers le milieu du 20ième, ces techniques furent adaptées par les travailleurs saisonniers qui utilisent du fil téléphonique recouvert d'isolant plastique.

Ursprünglich hatten Männer dekorative Muster für ihre Stöcke aus Messing- oder Kupferdraht gearbeitet. Mitte des 20. Jahrhunderts haben Wanderarbeiter diese Gestaltungsform verändert und aus plastikbezogenem Draht Gegenstände zum Verkauf hergestellt.

Acclaimed Ndebele muralists like Esther Mahlangu (*opposite, top*) and Francina Ndimande (*opposite bottom*) teach girls to paint on portable surfaces. Like their own more complex paintings, these works have found a market among local and foreign art collectors.

Esther Mahlangu et Francina Ndimande sont des artistes de réputation internationale qui enseignent aux jeunes filles la peinture sur surfaces amovibles. Bien que moins complexes que ceux de leurs maîtres, ces ouvrages se sont avérés très populaires.

International anerkannte Wandmaler der Ndebele, wie Esther Mahlangu und Francina Ndimande, zeigen den Mädchen, wie sie Malereien anfertigen können. Wie ihre eigenen, meist komplexeren Bildkompositionen, finden diese Schöpfungen guten Absatz.

Although some mural art forms have been adapted to serve new markets, this indigenous artistic tradition is still practised by many rural communities. The techniques and patterns used in the production of these murals vary considerably from one area to another.

Bien que certaines formes d'art mural aient été adaptées aux demandes de nouveaux marchés, cette tradition est toujours pratiquée par de nombreuses communautés. Le style de ces ouvrages varie sensiblement d'une région à l'autre.

Obwohl einige Wandmalereien den neuen Absatzmärkten angepaßt wurden, wird diese künstlerische Tradition weiterhin in vielen Landgemeinden gepflegt. Kunsttechnik und Motive der Wandmalereien unterscheiden sich merklich in den verschiedenen Gebieten.

Today, Ndebele women, such as Esther Mahlangu (*opposite*), often paint mural designs on commercially made pots. Some women are able to supplement the income they receive from their migrant husbands by selling works like these to exclusive outlets in cities like Johannesburg. But, since rural women also till the fields and take responsibility for most other household chores, few make a substantial living from activities of this kind.

Les femmes ndebeles, comme Esther Mahlangu (*ci-contre*), répètent souvent les motifs de leurs peintures murales sur des pots obtenus en commerce. Revendant leur ouvrage dans des magasins exclusifs en ville, comme à Johannesburg, certaines femmes savent ainsi suppléer au salaire de leur mari. Cependant, à cause du temps consacré aux corvées ménagères et à l'agriculture, ce revenu est rarement substantiel.

Heutzutage bemalen Frauen der Ndebele, wie Esther Mahlangu (*gegenüber*) oftmals fabrikmäßig hergestellte Töpfe mit den Mustern der Wandmalereien. Einige Frauen bessern ihr Einkommen, das von auswärts arbeitenden Ehemännern kommt, dadurch auf, daß sie solche Arbeiten an exklusive Geschäfte in Städten wie Johannesburg verkaufen. Da die Frauen auf dem Lande aber weiterhin die Feldarbeit und praktisch alle andere Hausarbeit verrichten, können nur wenige sich auf diesem Wege ein ertragreiches Einkommen sichern.

Like the designs Ndebele muralists paint on their homesteads, those produced for use on commercially manufactured plates are characterized by a reliance on starkly juxtaposed primary colours boldly outlined in black.

Comme les motifs que les artisans ndebeles peignent sur les murs de leurs propriétés, ceux qui sont appliqués sur les assiettes disponibles en commerce montrent le même contraste saisissant, créé par l'usage des couleurs primaires bordées de grosses lignes noires.

Genau wie die Muster, die von den Ndebele auf die Wände ihrer Heimstätten gemalt werden, zeigen auch die Bemalungen auf kommerziell erzeugten Tellern die charakteristischen kontrastreichen starken Farben mit dicken schwarzen Umrandungen.

The plates Ndebele women market are generally covered in abstract patterns, but a few include motifs resembling the double-storey houses and other symbols of material prosperity these women sometimes use to decorate homestead walls.

Les assiettes vendues par les femmes ndebeles sont généralement ornées de motifs abstraits. Mais on trouvera aussi des motifs représentant des maisons à étage, et autres symboles de prospérité que les femmes utilisent dans leurs peintures murales.

Im allgemeinen versehen die Ndebele-Frauen die zum Verkauf bestimmten Teller mit abstrakten Mustern, aber bei einigen kommen auch andere Motive vor, wie ein doppelstöckiges Haus und andere Symbole des Wohlstands, wie sie von den Frauen mitunter auf die Wände der Heimstätten gemalt werden.

Communities like the Bantwane often preserve old pots which are used for brewing beer. The value ascribed to these vessels lies mainly in the fact that beer plays an important role in rituals associated with the homestead's ancestors.

Les Bantwanes, comme d'autres communautés, préservent souvent d'anciens pots dans lesquels ils brassent de la bière. La valeur attribuée à ces récipients vient de ce que la bière joue un rôle important dans les rituels associés avec les ancêtres.

Volksgruppen wie die Bantwane bemühen sich oftmals um das Bewahren alter Töpfe, die zum Bierbrauen benutzt werden. Der Wert, den man diesen Gefäßen beimißt, beruht hauptsächlich auf der Bedeutung, die das Bier bei Riten im Zusammenhang mit den Ahnen der Heimstätte spielt.

The Nala family, most of whom live in a remote rural homestead in the Kranskop district of KwaZulu-Natal, has achieved international acclaim for their finely executed pots. Some are decorated with motifs taken from popular sources like Lion matchboxes.

La famille Nala, du district de Kranskop, une région reculée du KwaZulu-Natal, a atteint une réputation internationale pour l'excellence de ses pots. Certains sont ornés de motifs populaires, empruntés de marques comme les allumettes 'Lion'.

Die Nala-Familie, von der die Mehrheit in einer abgelegenen ländlichen Heimstätte im Bezirk von Kranskop in KwaZulu-Natal lebt, hat internationale Anerkennung erlangt für ihre kunstvoll gearbeiteten Töpfe. Manche sind mit allgemein bekannten Motiven dekoriert, wie man sie etwa auf den Etiketten von Streichholzschachteln sieht.

While large pots are generally used for brewing beer, people drink this beer from smaller vessels. On ritual occasions, these smaller pots are passed from one person to another, thus reinforcing the sense of community fostered by these occasions.

Les grands pots étant réservés à la fermentation de la bière, celle-ci est servie dans des récipients plus petits. Lors des occasions rituelles, les pots sont passés d'une personne à l'autre, renforçant ainsi le sens communautaire de ces occasions.

Zum Bierbrauen werden gewöhnlich große Töpfe benutzt, aber getrunken wird das Bier aus kleineren Gefäßen. Bei rituellen Anlässen werden diese kleineren Gefäße von einem zum anderen weitergereicht, wodurch das Zusammengehörigkeitsgefühl bei solchen Gelegenheiten noch verstärkt wird.

Rural women around South Africa commonly carry pots and other containers on their heads. Most of them learn the art of balancing surprisingly large vessels, which is done with the aid of scarves or woven grass rings, at a very early age from their mothers or other female relatives.

Dans les communautés rurales, les femmes portent habituellement les pots et autres récipients sur la tête. L'art d'équilibrer ces objets, dont les dimensions savent être respectables, est appris dès le plus jeune âge. La tâche est facilitée grâce à un coussin fait de foulards ou d'anneaux d'herbes tressées.

Die Frauen tragen Töpfe und andere Behälter auf dem Kopf. Meistens erlernen sie das Balancieren von erstaunlich großen Gefäßen, wenn sie noch sehr jung sind. Schals und geflochtene Strohkränze verschaffen Halt und Polsterung.

Many rural women grow gourds. Used as eating and drinking bowls or for storage, these gourds are often decorated with abstract patterns which vary in style from one community to another.

De nombreuses femmes cultivent des calebasses. Utilisées comme récipient pour boire, manger et garder la nourriture, ces calebasses sont souvent décorées de motifs abstraits dont le style varie d'une communauté à l'autre.

Viele Landfrauen pflanzen Flaschenkürbisse an. Ausgehöhlt, dienen sie als Eß- und Trinkgeschirr oder zum Aufbewahren von Vorräten. Sie werden oft mit abstrakten Mustern verziert, die von sich von Gebiet zu Gebiet unterscheiden.

In the past, large grass baskets were made to store various kinds of grain, but most contemporary examples are intended for outside buyers. These baskets generally differ in shape and size from those produced for indigenous use.

Dans le passé, on fabriquait de grands paniers d'herbes tressées pour entreposer diverses sortes de grains. De nos jours, la plupart sont destinés à la revente aux touristes. En général, ces paniers sont différents de ceux produits pour l'utilisation domestique.

Früher dienten die großen Körbe zum Aufbewahren von verschiedenen Getreidearten, aber die heutigen sind meist für auswärtige Käufer bestimmt. Solche Körbe unterscheiden sich gewöhnlich in Form und Größe von denen für den Hausgebrauch.

In present-day northern KwaZulu-Natal, women make colourful grass baskets for sale to exclusive shops in urban areas. Historically it was men who made grain baskets and the woven lids people still use to cover clay beer pots, but largely through the impact of migrant labour many of the art forms formerly associated with men are now practised by women.

Au KwaZulu-Natal, les femmes tressent des paniers aux couleurs vives qui seront revendus dans des magasins chics en ville. Historiquement, la fabrication des paniers de grain et le tressage des couvercles de pots de bière était l'apanage des hommes; mais le travail saisonnier causant l'exode des hommes vers la ville, ce sont les femmes qui mainterant pratiquent ces formes d'art.

Heutzutage flechten Frauen im nördlichen KwaZulu-Natal farbenfreudige Körbe zum Verkauf an exklusive Geschäfte in Stadtgebieten. Ursprünglich waren es die Männer, die Körbe zum Speichern von Getreide und Deckel für die Biertöpfe anfertigten, aber hauptsächlich durch die Wanderarbeit bedingt, werden jetzt viele Kunst- und Handarbeiten, die früher Männersache waren, von Frauen ausgeübt.

Materials like clay and grass are still used to this day to make the pots, brooms and baskets traditionally found in rural homesteads. When items intended primarily for this indigenous market are sold to outside buyers, they are often far more colourful than the household and other objects that craft specialists make for the day-to-day requirements of local consumers.

Des matériaux traditionnels comme la glaise et les herbes sèches, sont encore utilisés de nos jours dans les régions rurales pour la fabrication de pots et de balais. Quand de tels objets, destinés de prime abord pour usage domestique sont revendus à des tiers, ils sont souvent beaucoup plus ornementés que ceux fabriqués par les artisans pour les tâches ménagères.

Bis auf den heutigen Tag werden Ton und Stroh verwendet, um die Töpfe, Körbe und Besen, die man in den ländlichen Heimstätten antrifft, herzustellen. Wenn solche Artikel, die ursprünglich nur für den einheimischen Markt angefertigt wurden, für auswärtige Käufer produziert werden, sind sie häufig viel farbenfreudiger als die Haushaltswaren und andere Dinge, die für den Alltagsgebrauch der lokalen Bevölkerung gearbeitet werden.

Grass is also used in making various objects related to initiation. Among the South Sotho, for example, female initiates learn to make woven grass masks which they usually decorate with beadwork or tufts of wool. In the past, the skills used in the production of masks of this kind played a crucial role in the education of young girls.

Les herbes tressées sont aussi utilisées pour la fabrication d'objets liés à l'initiation. Par exemple, les initiées du South Sotho apprennent à tisser des masques qu'elles décoreront avec des perles et des touffes de laine. Dans le passé, l'enseignement des techniques nécessaires à la fabrication de masques de cette sorte prenait une place importante dans l'éducation des jeunes filles.

Stroh wird auch benutzt für die Anfertigung verschiedener Artikel für die Initiation. Bei den Süd-Sotho, beispielsweise, lernen die weiblichen Initianden Strohmasken zu flechten, die dann meistens mit Perlen und Wolltupfern verziert werden. In der Vergangenheit spielten die Fertigkeiten, die zu der Herstellung solcher Masken benötigt werden, eine wichtige Rolle in der Schulung der jungen Mädchen.

Like the production of grass masks, the art of body painting is associated with important ritual occasions. Some of the motifs that are used by South Sotho female initiates to decorate their bodies resemble the flower-like patterns married women paint on their homes. In most cases, there is a sense of balance in the relationship between these decorations and the contours of the body.

Comme la fabrication des masques d'herbes, l'art de décorer à même la peau est associé avec d'importants rituels. Certains des motifs à fleurs utilisés par les initiées du South Sotho ressemblent à ceux que les femmes peignent sur leurs maisons. Souvent le style du motif s'harmonise parfaitement avec les lignes du corps.

Genau wie die Herstellung von Strohmasken steht Körperbemalung im Zusammenhang mit bedeutenden rituellen Anlässen. Einige der Muster, mit denen Süd-Sotho Initianden ihre Körper verzieren, ähneln den blumenförmigen Motiven, mit denen verheiratete Frauen ihr Heim dekorieren. In den meisten Fällen besteht eine Harmonie zwischen den Bemalungen und den Körperkonturen.

South Sotho female initiates celebrate their willingness to enter the world of adult responsibility by wearing vibrant facial paints at their coming-out ceremonies. The colours used on these occasions are enhanced by the addition of petroleum jelly.

Lors des cérémonies d'initiation, les initiées du South Soto célèbrent leur intention d'accepter les responsabilités de l'âge adulte en se peignant le visage de couleurs vives. L'effet des fards utilisés dans ces occasions est renforcé par l'usage de vaseline.

Um ihre Bereitschaft zum Eintritt in die Erwachsenenwelt zu feiern, tragen Initianden der Süd-Sotho bunte Gesichtsmalereien bei ihrer Einführungszeremonie. Die Farben treten durch Beifügung von Vaseline kräftiger hervor.

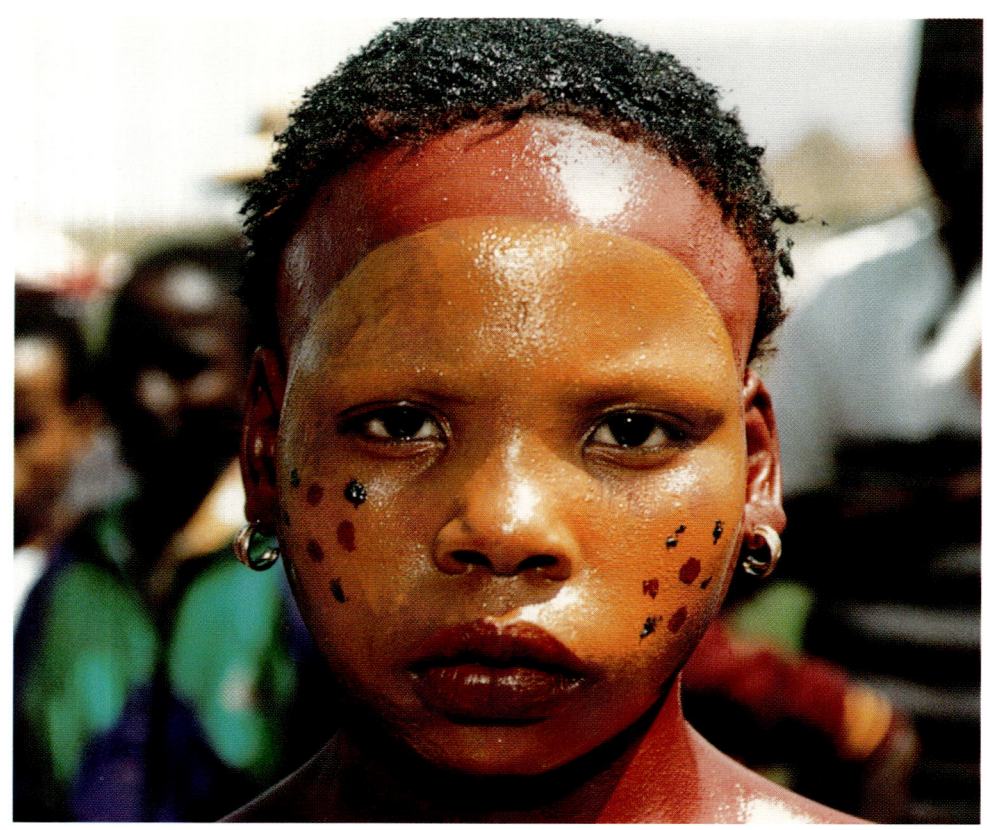

Wild furs are among the indigenous materials used in the production of clothing worn on special occasions, like that worn by Zulu king Goodwill Zwelethini and Chief Mangosuthu Buthelezi (above, left to right). Before restrictions on hunting, these furs were prepared by craft specialists, but today they are generally purchased from licensed merchants.

La fourrure est un des matériaux indigènes utilisés dans la fabrication de costumes pour occasions spéciales. Avant l'introduction de la chasse réglementée, les peaux étaient préparées par des spécialistes, de nos jours elles sont obtenues en commerce.

Wildpelze werden für die Anfertigung von Kleidung für besondere Anlässe gebraucht. Bevor es Jagdschutzgesetze gab, wurden sie von sogenannten Spezialisten gearbeitet, aber heute kauft man sie von Händlern, die eine entsprechende Handelsgenehmigung haben.

In the past people commonly wore karosses to protect themselves against the winter cold. Since the introduction of commercially produced blankets in the course of the 19th century the practice of tanning skins for this purpose has virtually been lost.

Dans le passé on se couvrait de *karos* (peau d'animal) pour se protéger du froid hivernal. Depuis l'introduction de la couverture au cours du 19ième, la pratique de tanner des peaux d'animaux pour cet usage a été virtuellement abandonnée.

Früher trugen die Menschen gewöhnlich Fellumhänge, um sich gegen die Winterkälte zu schützen. Seit im Laufe des 19. Jahrhunderts kommerziell hergestellte Decken in Umlauf kamen, ist das Gerben der Felle für diesen Zweck praktisch verlorengegangen.

Today, leather garments are made mainly for use on ritual occasions like initiation ceremonies. The overall texture and softness of aprons and other forms of dress made from these skins depends in part on whether people use hides obtained from goats or cattle. While the leather garments worn by women are generally made by female craft specialists, male specialists usually sew the wild animal skins that are more commonly worn by men.

De nos jours les costumes en peau ne sont fabriqués que pour des occasions rituelles, comme les cérémonies d'initiation. La texture et la souplesse des tabliers et autres vêtements varient selon qu'il s'agit d'une peau de chèvre ou de vache. Alors que les costumes de peaux portés par les femmes sont généralement cousus par des artisanes, ce sont des artisans qui fabriquent ceux portés par les hommes.

Kleidungsstücke aus Leder werden heute hauptsächlich für rituelle Anlässe wie Initiationszeremonien angefertigt. Beschaffenheit und Schmiegsamkeit der Schürzen und anderer Bekleidungsstücke aus Fellen hängt teilweise davon ab, ob die Häute von Ziegen oder von Rindern stammen. Ledergewänder für Frauen werden generell auch von Frauen angefertigt, während solche, die von Männern getragen werden, auch von männlichen Fellverarbeitern hergestellt werden.

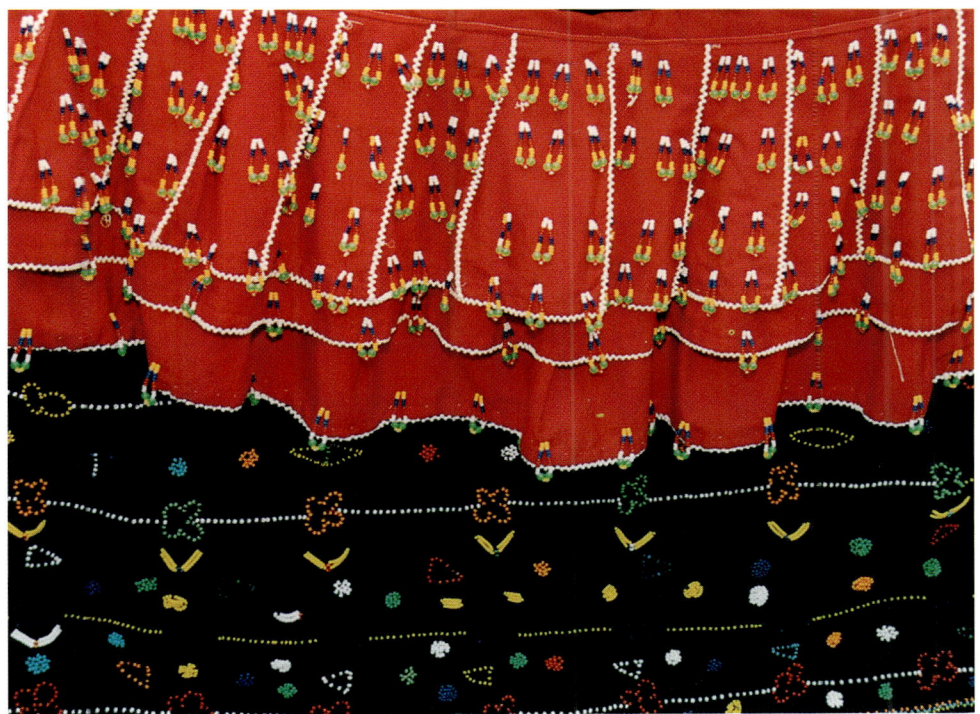

Following the widespread introduction of imported cotton in the course of the 19th century rural women have been enthusiastic sewers. Although many now use manual sewing machines, the techniques employed in the production of various kinds of garments is often extremely time-consuming.

L'importation du coton au cours du 19ième fut un grand succès, et les femmes de la campagne sont rapidement devenues avides de couture. Bien qu'elles soient nombreuses à avoir adopté la machine à coudre, certaines des techniques utilisées dans la production de vêtements prennent souvent beaucoup de temps.

Nach der weit verbreiteten Einführung importierter Baumwolle im Laufe des 19. Jahrhunderts entwickelten sich die Landfrauen zu begeisterten Näherinnen. Obwohl viele jetzt handbetriebene Nähmaschinen benutzen, ist die Anfertigung der verschiedenen Kleidungsstücke oft sehr zeitaufwendig.

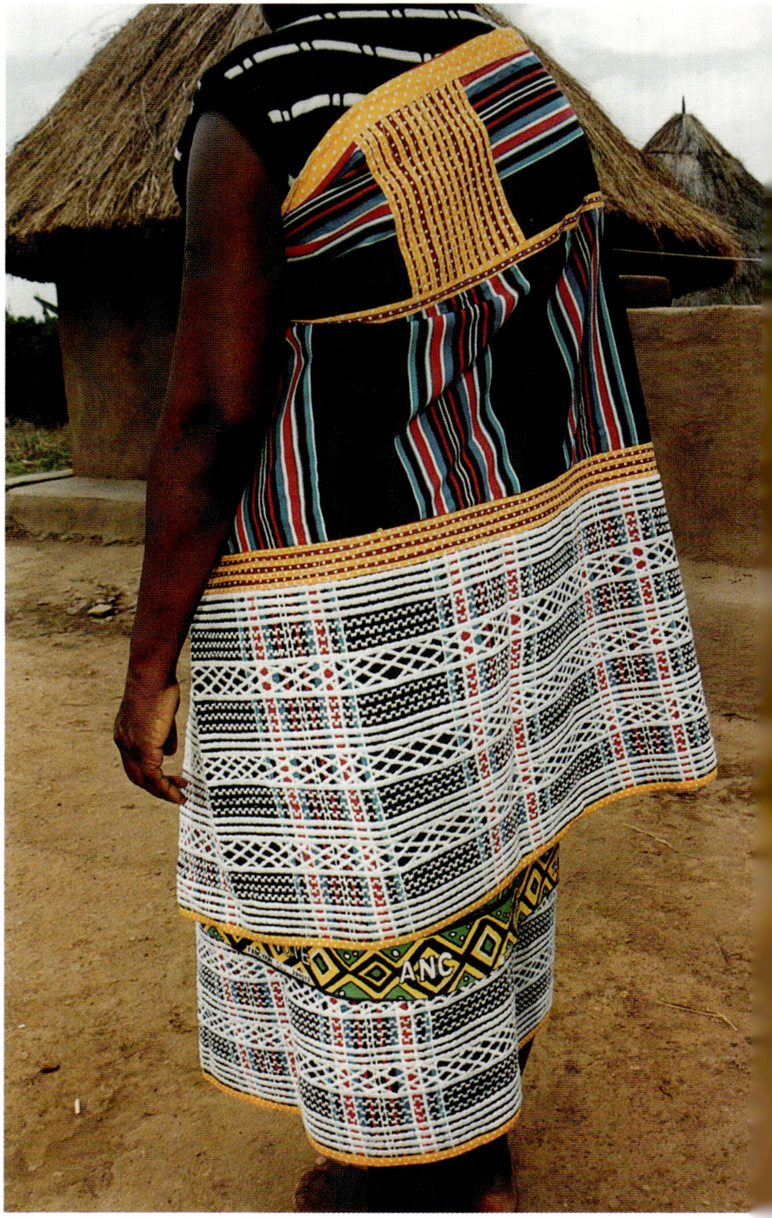

76

Although cloths and blankets are often adapted, for example through the addition of braiding and safety pins, some communities like the Venda (*opposite*) and Swazi (*below*) now wear commercially manufactured cloths intended specifically for these markets.

Bien que les étoffes et les couvertures soient souvent particularisées par l'addition d'accessoires, notamment de galons et d'épingles de sûreté, certaines communautés comme les Vendas (*ci-contre*) et les Swazis (*ci-dessous*) s'habillent d'étoffes imprimées spécialement fabriquées à leur intention.

Stoffe und Decken werden häufig etwa durch das Anbringen von Borten und Sicherheitsnadeln zweckentsprechend angepaßt, aber manche Volksgruppen wie die Venda (*gegenüber*) und die Swazi (*unten*) tragen jetzt Stoffe, die eigens für diesen Markt produziert werden.

Ndebele women wear a great variety of beadwork and other forms of adornment on special occasions. The materials they use to produce this clothing is often remarkably inventive. Like Zulu women (*see* pages 80-81), they commonly make richly decorated ornaments with the aid of metal studs. In addition to this, these Ndebele women often modify hats and caps purchased from stores by adding beadwork and other details to them.

Les femmes ndebeles portent une grande diversité d'ornements perlés et autres parures pour les occasions spéciales. Le choix des matériaux qu'elles utilisent surprend souvent par sa créativité. Comme les zouloues (*voir* pages 80-81), elles produisent des objets richement ornés de clous. De plus, ces femmes ndebeles souvent changeront l'aspect d'une casquette ou d'un chapeau trouvé en commerce, en y ajoutant des perles et d'autres éléments ad hoc.

Die Frauen der Ndebele tragen eine große Auswahl an Perlenarbeiten und anderem schmückenden Beiwerk zu besonderen Anlässen. Was sie alles für ihre Garderobe verwenden, zeugt von großem Einfallsreichtum. Wie die Zulufrauen (*siehe* Seite 80-81) fertigen sie reich verzierte Ornamente mit Nieten an. Hüte und Kappen aus dem Handel werden durch Perlenarbeit und andere Details verändert.

79

Historically Bantwane women made beaded head ornaments for ritual occasions, but it has now become increasingly common for them to adapt found objects like coins, the metal accessories from cars and plastic hairpins for this purpose.

Les femmes bantwanes fabriquaient des coiffes de perles pour les occasions rituelles, mais il est devenu courant de les voir utiliser des objets communs, tels que des pièces de monnaie, des épingles à cheveux en plastique et des accessoires automobiles.

Von Alters her fertigten die Frauen der Bantwane Kopfschmuck aus Perlen an, aber es kommt jetzt immer häufiger vor, daß sie auch Fundstücke wie Münzen, Metallteile von Autos und Haarnadeln aus Plastik zu diesem Zweck verwenden.

In contrast to most communities where the use of beadwork is becoming less common, especially among younger men, traditional healers continue to make their own beaded garments. This practice is still prevalent with both male and female healers.

Contrairement aux communautés où les ornements perlés deviennent plus rares, les guérisseurs continuent de fabriquer leurs propres costumes perlés. Cette pratique est toujours répandue chez tous les guérisseurs, tant hommes que femmes.

Im Gegensatz zu dem allgemeinen Rückgang in der Verwendung von Perlenarbeiten, besonders bei jungen Männern, fertigen Heilkundige weiterhin Bekleidungsstücke für sich aus Perlen an. Dies gilt sowohl für weibliche, als auch für männliche Heilkundige.

86

Throughout South Africa young unmarried women and newly married women remain major consumers of beadwork which they wear on ritual occasions like coming-out ceremonies and following momentous events like the birth of children. In many cases, girls learn to make their own beadwork at a very early age, generally under the supervision of their mothers, most of whom are able to teach their daughters a variety of beadwork techniques.

Les jeunes sud africaines sont d'importantes consommatrices de perles dont elles se parent lors d'occasions spéciales, comme les cérémonies de débutantes ou encore pour célébrer la naissance d'un enfant. Dans de nombreux cas, elles apprennent à utiliser les perles dès le plus jeune âge, généralement sous la supervision de leur mère, qui souvent a maîtrisé une grande diversité de techniques.

In ganz Südafrika tragen unverheiratete junge Frauen und die Jungvermählten weiterhin viel Perlenschmuck, den sie zu rituellen Anlässen wie Einführungszeremonien und nach bedeutenden Ereignissen wie Geburten anlegen. Sehr oft lernen die Mädchen schon in jungen Jahren, sich ihren eigenen Perlenschmuck anzufertigen. Meist geschieht dies unter Anleitung der Mütter, von denen die meisten ihren Töchtern verschiedene Macharten für Perlenarbeiten beibringen können.

Among the Ndebele (*above*), and Bantwane and Bakôpa (*opposite*), married women still tend to produce their own beadwork. But today many use this skill more commonly to make jewellery and other items for outside buyers.

Chez les Ndebeles, Bantwanes et Bakôpas, les femmes mariées fabriquent généralement elles-mêmes leurs ornements de perles. Aujourd'hui elles sont nombreuses à utiliser leurs talents pour produire des ornements et autres objets destinés à la revente.

Verheiratete Frauen der Ndebele, Bantwane und Bakôpa fertigen häufig noch Perlenarbeiten für den eigenen Gebrauch an. Aber heute wird dieses Können mehr darauf verwandt, Schmuck und andere Artikel für auswärtige Käufer herzustellen.

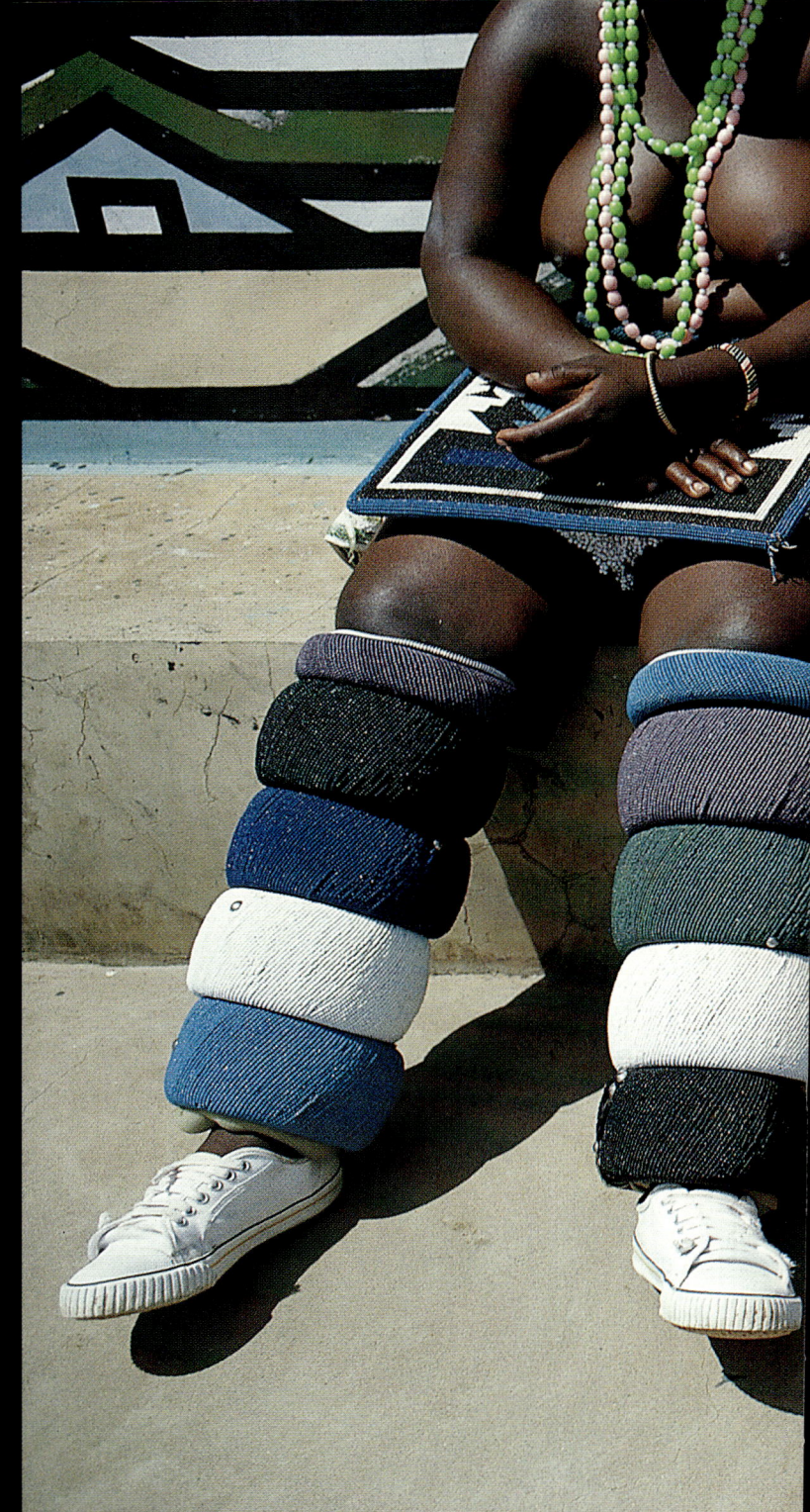

Long hours are spent making beadwork items worn on ritual occasions. While the production of some pieces involves the use of comparatively simple beading techniques, the completion of others requires a great deal of thought and effort. Should they run out of time or the money needed to buy beads, most women improvise by using plastic and other materials.

De longues heures sont consacrées à la fabrication d'ornements perlés pour les occasions rituelles. Alors que certaines pièces sont relativement faciles à produire, d'autres exigent beaucoup d'application et de soin. Si on devait tomber à court de temps ou d'argent pour acheter des perles, on improviserait, utilisant les matériaux disponibles, comme des objets en plastique.

Viele Arbeitsstunden werden darauf verwendet, Perlenartikel anzufertigen, die zu rituellen Anlässen getragen werden. Während einige eine verhältnismäßig einfache Machart haben, erfordern andere viel Mühe und Geschicklichkeit. Sollte ihnen die Zeit knapp werden oder das Geld zum Ankauf weiterer Perlen ausgehen, improvisieren die meisten Frauen mit Plastik und anderen Materialien.

With the exception of male diviners, men never make their own beadwork. Those who have gone through initiation rely on their mothers to provide them with gifts of this kind, which they wear at their coming-out ceremonies. Among the South Sotho there are considerable variations in the decoration of these beadwork pieces.

Excepté pour les devins, les hommes ne fabriquent jamais leurs propres ornements de perles. Ceux qui ont été initiés reçoivent leurs ornements en cadeau de leur mère, ornements qu'ils porteront lors des cérémonies marquant la fin des célébrations. Chez les South Sotho on trouve une grande diversité de styles dans les ornements.

Mit Ausnahme der männlichen Heilkundigen, fertigen Männer nie ihre eigenen Perlenarbeiten an. Diejenigen, die an Mannbarkeitsriten teilgenommen haben, verlassen sich darauf, daß ihre Mütter ihnen welche schenken, die sie dann bei ihrer Einführungszeremonie tragen. Bei den Süd-Sotho weisen solche Perlenarbeiten eine große Vielfalt dekorativer Elemente auf.

94

Since the mid-1970s, when local dealers began to promote the work of rural beadmakers, it has become common for museums and private collectors to display the beautifully beaded blankets made by Ndebele women alongside paintings by fine artists. The recognition afforded these beadmakers is consistent with the fact that art lovers no longer endorse earlier distinctions between notions of art and craft.

Quand, vers le milieu des années 70, les marchands d'œuvres d'art commencèrent à promouvoir l'ouvrage des artisans ruraux, les musées et collecteurs privés exposèrent les splendides couvertures ornées de perles faites par les femmes ndebeles, côte à côte avec les œuvres d'artistes renommés. La reconnaissance du talent de ces femmes correspond avec l'opinion des amateurs d'art qui ne font plus de distinction entre l'art et l'artisanat.

Seit Mitte der 1970er Jahre, als Händler im Land anfingen die Handarbeiten der Perlenarbeiter auf dem Lande zu vermarkten, wurde es üblich, in Museen und Privatkollektionen die wunderschön gearbeiteten Perlendecken der Ndebele-Frauen neben Gemälden von namhaften Künstlern auszustellen. Die Anerkennung, die diesen Perlenarbeitern gezollt wird, steht im Einklang mit der Tatsache, daß bei Kunstliebhabern nicht mehr die früheren Abgrenzungen zwischen Kunst und Handwerk gelten.

The beaded blankets traditionally made by Ndebele artists are still worn on special occasions. Decorated with distinctive patterns similar to those found on Ndebele mural paintings, they are now worn together with accessories such as mirrors. These hybrid dress styles, adopted by women since the mid-19th century, underline the remarkable creativity and inventiveness of traditionalists living in rural South Africa.

Les traditionnelles couvertures ornées de perles des artistes ndebeles sont encore portées lors d'occasions spéciales. Recouvertes de motifs caractéristiques semblables à ceux de leurs peintures murales, on y ajoute des accessoires comme des miroirs. Ces costumes, dont le style disparate remonte au 19ième, témoignent de la créativité et de l'ingéniosité des traditionalistes ruraux de l'Afrique du Sud.

Die mit Perlen bestickten Decken der Ndebele werden bei besonderen Anlässen immer noch getragen. Dekoriert mit einschlägigen Motiven, ähnlich denen der Wandmalereien, werden sie heute zusammen mit Beifügungen wie Spiegeln getragen. Diese Stilverbindungen bei der Bekleidung, die von den Frauen Mitte des 19. Jahrhunderts eingeführt wurden, betonen die bemerkenswerte Kreativität und den Einfallsreichtum der Traditionalisten überall in den Landgemeinden Südafrikas.